SEX EDUCATION

The Muslim perspective

1994 update

(Includes the latest changes arising from the 1993 Education Act)

Ghulam Sarwar

THE MUSLIM EDUCATIONAL TRUST

Sex Education

Formal sex education has been part of a broad and balanced school curriculum for a long time, but the Education (No. 2) Act 1986 gave school governors the option of deciding whether sex education should be offered in their school or not. The Education Act 1993 (Section 241[1]) removes that option for secondary schools, for whose pupils sex education is now compulsory. As far as the content of sex education lessons is concerned, Section 241(2) amends the 1944 Act to include education about AIDS, HIV and sexually transmitted diseases in the definition of sex education. **However, the same act (Section 241[3]) amends the ERA to allow parents of pupils in primary and secondary schools to withdraw their children from all or part of sex education in the school, unless it forms part of the National Curriculum. Any sex education which forms part of science within the National Curriculum must be limited to "biological aspects". (Section 241[4][c])**

Hence, the fears held by many parents – not just Muslims – that their children would be forced to learn about AIDS and how it is transmitted and study objectionable material can be allayed by taking advantage of the right to withdraw.

Muslims are not against sex education *per se*. Islam encourages all purposeful human actions, and this includes sex education as part of a broad and balanced curriculum to prepare young people as responsible citizens. What Islam not only discourages but also prohibits is the promotion of obscenity, irresponsibility and shameful acts which debase human beings. If sex education is taught in accordance with the requirements of the Education (No. 2) Act 1986, that is within the context of family life and morality (section 46), most Muslim parents would have no objections. However, the 1993 Education Act makes it clear that secondary school pupils must study sex education (unless they have been withdrawn by their parents) including education on AIDS, HIV and other sexually transmitted diseases. This may make Muslim parents think twice before allowing their children to participate in such lessons.

Religious viewpoints on extramarital relationships, contraception, abortion and homosexuality (all of which feature in sex education programmes) should be included in the sex education policy of schools.

It is wrong to include in a programme of sex education material which parents consider to be obscene and objectionable. Schools should consult with parents and the local community. In fact, governors of

SEX EDUCATION

The Muslim perspective

1994 update

(Includes the latest changes arising from the 1993 Education Act)

Ghulam Sarwar

THE MUSLIM EDUCATIONAL TRUST

Sex Education

Formal sex education has been part of a broad and balanced school curriculum for a long time, but the Education (No. 2) Act 1986 gave school governors the option of deciding whether sex education should be offered in their school or not. The Education Act 1993 (Section 241[1]) removes that option for secondary schools, for whose pupils sex education is now compulsory. As far as the content of sex education lessons is concerned, Section 241(2) amends the 1944 Act to include education about AIDS, HIV and sexually transmitted diseases in the definition of sex education. **However, the same act (Section 241[3]) amends the ERA to allow parents of pupils in primary and secondary schools to withdraw their children from all or part of sex education in the school, unless it forms part of the National Curriculum. Any sex education which forms part of science within the National Curriculum must be limited to "biological aspects". (Section 241[4][c])**

Hence, the fears held by many parents – not just Muslims – that their children would be forced to learn about AIDS and how it is transmitted and study objectionable material can be allayed by taking advantage of the right to withdraw.

Muslims are not against sex education *per se*. Islam encourages all purposeful human actions, and this includes sex education as part of a broad and balanced curriculum to prepare young people as responsible citizens. What Islam not only discourages but also prohibits is the promotion of obscenity, irresponsibility and shameful acts which debase human beings. If sex education is taught in accordance with the requirements of the Education (No. 2) Act 1986, that is within the context of family life and morality (section 46), most Muslim parents would have no objections. However, the 1993 Education Act makes it clear that secondary school pupils must study sex education (unless they have been withdrawn by their parents) including education on AIDS, HIV and other sexually transmitted diseases. This may make Muslim parents think twice before allowing their children to participate in such lessons.

Religious viewpoints on extramarital relationships, contraception, abortion and homosexuality (all of which feature in sex education programmes) should be included in the sex education policy of schools.

It is wrong to include in a programme of sex education material which parents consider to be obscene and objectionable. Schools should consult with parents and the local community. In fact, governors of both primary and secondary maintained schools are "required to have regard to any representations" made in this regard by the local community. In particular, advice from "religious groups" is to be taken into account when considering the school's sex education policy (DFE Draft Circular on Sex Education, para. 17); "due consideration" should also be given to "religious or cultural factors bearing on the discussion of sexual issues." (*Ibid.*, para. 10)

The MET always advises Muslim parents to make every effort to study the sex education policy in their children's schools; they should not ignore invitations to view such material prior to it being shown to their children. This is essential if the wishes of Muslim parents are to be taken into consideration by those responsible for their children's education.

Withdrawal requests from sex education lessons should be respected and the children given alternative academic work for the duration of the lesson.

Education Act 1993

Section 241

(2) In section 114(1) of the Education Act 1944 (interpretation), after the definition of "Senior pupil" there is inserted—

""Sex education" includes education about—

(a) Acquired Immune Deficiency Syndrome and Human Immunodeficiency Virus, and

(b) any other sexually transmitted disease".

(3) After section 17 of the Education Reform Act 1988 there is inserted—

"Exemption from sex education — *17A If the parent of any pupil in attendance at any maintained school requests that he may be wholly or partly excused from receiving sex education at the school, the pupil shall, except so far as such education is comprised in the National Curriculum, be so excused accordingly until the request is withdrawn."*

(4) The Secretary of State shall so exercise the power conferred by section 4 of that Act to revise the National Curriculum as to secure that the subject of science does not include—

(a) Acquired Immune Deficiency Syndrome and Human Immunodeficiency Virus,

(b) any other sexually transmitted disease, or

(c) aspects of human sexual behaviour, other than biological aspects ...

DFE Draft Circular on Sex Education, 6th December 1993

10. In primary schools, care must be taken to match any sex education provided to the maturity of the pupils involved, which may not always correspond to their chronological age. It should take account both of their capacity to absorb sensitive information and of the extent to which it is essential for them to have such information at that point in their development. At this stage, the aim should be to prepare pupils to cope with the physical and emotional challenges of growing up, and to give them an elementary understanding of human reproduction. Pupils' questions should be answered sensitively and with due consideration for any particular religious or cultural factors bearing on the discussion of sexual issues.

17. In discharging their duties relating to sex education, governors must take such steps as are reasonably practicable to ensure that any provision they make accords with the requirement of section 46 of the Education (No. 2) Act 1986 that it should encourage pupils to have due regard to moral considerations and the value of family life. They are also required to have regard to any representations made to them by anyone connected with the community served by the school. Governors will wish to take due account of representations or advice they may receive from health authorities and from others, in particular religious groups and ethnic minority communities ...

Rajab 1414
January 1994

A supplement to Sex Education – The Muslim Perspective

The Muslim Educational Trust

130 Stroud Green Road, London N4 3RZ

both primary and secondary maintained schools are "required to have regard to any representations" made in this regard by the local community. In particular, advice from "religious groups" is to be taken into account when considering the school's sex education policy (DFE Draft Circular on Sex Education, para. 17); "due consideration" should also be given to "religious or cultural factors bearing on the discussion of sexual issues." (*Ibid.*, para. 10)

The MET always advises Muslim parents to make every effort to study the sex education policy in their children's schools; they should not ignore invitations to view such material prior to it being shown to their children. This is essential if the wishes of Muslim parents are to be taken into consideration by those responsible for their children's education.

Withdrawal requests from sex education lessons should be respected and the children given alternative academic work for the duration of the lesson.

Education Act 1993

Section 241

(2) In section 114(1) of the Education Act 1944 (interpretation), after the definition of "Senior pupil" there is inserted—

""Sex education" includes education about—

(a) Acquired Immune Deficiency Syndrome and Human Immunodeficiency Virus, and

(b) any other sexually transmitted disease".

(3) After section 17 of the Education Reform Act 1988 there is inserted—

"Exemption from sex education — *17A If the parent of any pupil in attendance at any maintained school requests that he may be wholly or partly excused from receiving sex education at the school, the pupil shall, except so far as such education is comprised in the National Curriculum, be so excused accordingly until the request is withdrawn."*

(4) The Secretary of State shall so exercise the power conferred by section 4 of that Act to revise the National Curriculum as to secure that the subject of science does not include—

(a) Acquired Immune Deficiency Syndrome and Human Immunodeficiency Virus,

(b) any other sexually transmitted disease, or

(c) *aspects of human sexual behaviour, other than biological aspects ...*

DFE Draft Circular on Sex Education, 6th December 1993

10. In primary schools, care must be taken to match any sex education provided to the maturity of the pupils involved, which may not always correspond to their chronological age. It should take account both of their capacity to absorb sensitive information and of the extent to which it is essential for them to have such information at that point in their development. At this stage, the aim should be to prepare pupils to cope with the physical and emotional challenges of growing up, and to give them an elementary understanding of human reproduction. Pupils' questions should be answered sensitively and with due consideration for any particular religious or cultural factors bearing on the discussion of sexual issues.

17. In discharging their duties relating to sex education, governors must take such steps as are reasonably practicable to ensure that any provision they make accords with the requirement of section 46 of the Education (No. 2) Act 1986 that it should encourage pupils to have due regard to moral considerations and the value of family life. They are also required to have regard to any representations made to them by anyone connected with the community served by the school. Governors will wish to take due account of representations or advice they may receive from health authorities and from others, in particular religious groups and ethnic minority communities ...

Rajab 1414
January 1994

A supplement to Sex Education – The Muslim Perspective
The Muslim Educational Trust
130 Stroud Green Road, London N4 3RZ

SEX EDUCATION

The Muslim perspective

Ghulam Sarwar

THE MUSLIM EDUCATIONAL TRUST

1st edition September 1989
2nd, revised, edition December 1992

Edited by:
Ibrahim Hewitt

ISBN 0 907261 26 4

British Library Cataloguing-in-Publication Data.
A catalogue record for this book is
available from the British Library.

Published by:
The Muslim Educational Trust
130 Stroud Green Road
London N4 3RZ
Tel: 071 272 8502
Fax: 071 281 3457

Printed by Printhaüs Graphique,
Round Spinney, Northampton.

Contents

In the name of Allah, The Most Merciful, The Most Kind

Preface to the first edition

All praise is for Allah (God), the Creator and Sustainer of the universe Who, by His infinite Mercy, has provided for all the needs of His creatures.

The Muslim Educational Trust (MET), established in 1966, is a pioneering organisation set up to cater for the educational needs of Muslims in the UK. It is the only national Muslim organisation which sends Islamic teachers to maintained schools in England to teach Islam, *in English*, to Muslim children within school premises under the provisions of the education legislation.

Sex education has been part of the school curriculum for a long time, but the Education (No. 2) Act, 1986 has highlighted it: now, school governors must include it in the school curriculum within the context of family life and morality (sections 46, 17 & 18 of the Education [No. 2] Act, 1986). Section 28 of the Local Government Act also an important effect on sex education, particularly relating to homosexuality.

I have made a modest attempt in this booklet to explain the Muslim view-point on sex education. My aim was to focus precisely on the Islamic view-point concerning sexual relationships.

The booklet is mainly intended to inform Muslim parents, head teachers, Local Education Authorities and all who deal with the concerns of Muslims on sex education. I hope they will find this small contribution helpful. All suggestions on the booklet will be welcome. I implore Allah Almighty to accept my humble efforts; Amin!

London
Safar, 1410 AH
September, 1989 CE

Ghulam Sarwar
Director
The Muslim Educational Trust

In the name of Allah, The Most Merciful, The Most kind

Preface to the second, revised edition

Alhamdulillah (all praise is for Allah), my book *Sex Education: The Muslim Perspective* was well-received by parents and professionals alike. It was the first book which set out to explain the Islamic viewpoint on the issue of sex education in schools. The permissiveness of the sixties, the gradual changes in attitudes towards sex that followed and the horrors of HIV and AIDS have highlighted the importance of such education. However, the manner and content used in sex education is still largely controversial.

The demand for this small book has motivated me to almost completely re-write it in an effort to make the Islamic viewpoint clearer on the issue of sex and sexuality. I am grateful to my colleague *Ibrahim Hewitt* who has edited the text and made some useful improvements.

As with the first edition, any comments and/or suggestions will be most welcome.

I implore Almighty Allah to accept my humble efforts and grant me a pardon in the Akhirah (life after death). Amin.

London
Jumada Al-Thani 1413 AH
December 1992 CE

Ghulam Sarwar
Director
The Muslim Educational Trust

Introduction

Education is the process by which children are prepared for life. It aims for the development of the complete personality of a child. The Education Reform Act, 1988 (ERA) states that children in maintained schools have to be educated through a *balanced and broadly based curriculum* which

(a) *Promotes the spiritual, moral, cultural, mental and physical development of pupils at the school and of society; and*

(b) *Prepares such pupils for the opportunities, responsibilities and experiences of adult life.* [Sec. 1 (2)(a)(b)]

When education is regarded as a complete concept it is obvious that sex should be included since it is an important aspect of human life.

Section 46 of the Education (No 2) Act 1986 requires that:

"The local education authority by whom any county, voluntary or special school is maintained, and the governing body and head teacher of the school, shall take such steps as are reasonably practicable to secure that where sex education is given to any registered pupils at the school it is given in such a manner as to encourage those pupils to have due regard to moral considerations and the value of family life."

Islam encompasses every aspect of life and all human actions should be directed towards the attainment of Allah's pleasure in order to be rewarded in this life and in the life hereafter (the *Akhirah*):

Say: Truly, my prayer and my service of sacrifice, my life and my death are (all) for Allah, the Cherisher of the worlds...
Al-Qur'an, chapter 6, verse 162

Our Lord! Give us good in this world and good in the hereafter, and save us from the torment of the fire.
Al-Qur'an, chapter 2, verse 201

Pursuit of knowledge is an obligation on every Muslim, male and female, and this knowledge must prepare a person to be a worthy servant of Allah. All human beings are judged by Allah according to their piety (*Taqwa*).

"Seeking knowledge is obligatory on all Muslims."

Sahih Muslim

I created the jinn and humankind only that they might worship Me.

Al-Qur'an, chapter 51, verse 56

... Lo! the best among you in the sight of Allah is the best in taqwa. Lo! Allah is Knower, Aware.

Al-Qur'an, chapter 49, verse 13

A Muslim must live according to the tenets of Islam as the vicegerent (*Khalifah*) of Allah on earth; all human actions must be guided by Allah's commands as contained in the Qur'an and as demonstrated by the life example (*Sunnah*) of Prophet Muhammad (may Allah's peace and blessings be upon him).

This is the framework within which education - including sex education - for Muslim children must fit. We are a long way, though, from seeing this happen in the British education system.

British society is, to all intents and purposes, secular and materialistic in outlook, and matters such as "the spiritual and moral" aspects of life remain largely ignored or marginalised in terms of the actual curriculum applied in schools, contrary to the objective set in section 2 of the ERA.

Muslim parents, therefore, face problems in this respect. Although they have to recognise that they cannot achieve an ideal solution to the educational problems faced by their children, it is possible to solve at least some of them by co-operating with other parents. A number of the concerns Muslims have in education matters are held in common with many non-Muslims: the deteriorating quality of education; increasing levels of truancy, violence and undisciplined behaviour in schools; a decline in the standards of morality and decency. By coming together in co-operation with others, Muslim parents can counter some of the undesirable and un-Islamic things going on in schools today. Since this is a democratic society it is possible for Muslim parents to air their views - within the framework of the law - and for these views to be given due consideration.

One of the main concerns of Muslim parents is not, as is commonly supposed, sex education *per se*. The need for sex education is not doubted, especially when permissiveness and liberalised social attitudes have led to early sexual experimentation resulting in increasing numbers of abortions, schoolgirl mothers, family stress, illegitimate children and one-parent families. Rather, Muslims feel that the methodology and content used to teach this sensitive subject contravenes Islamic teachings and the debate centres on where, how and by whom sex education is to be given. Some are of the opinion that the parents are responsible whilst others consider the school to be better suited. Wherever it is given, however, it is important for Muslims that the principles of Islam are not broken in any way.

Family life, with marriage at the core and care for both children and parents as a basic tenet, is strongly recommended in Islam. Sex education must be looked at with this concept firmly in mind: without such a holistic outlook it will be almost impossible to fully understand Islamic teachings. Nothing prescribed in Islam is aimless and human sexuality is no exception.

N.B. References from the collections of the Prophet's sayings (*Ahadith*, plural of *Hadith*) have been taken from the following: *Sahih Al-Bukhari, Sahih Muslim, Sunan Abu Dawud, Sunan Ibn Majah, Jami' At-Tirmidhi, Sunan An-Nasa'i* and *Al-Muwatta* of Imam Malik.

The Islamic attitude to sexual relationships

Islam is very practical and gives guidance for all aspects of life, including sexuality. Marriage is regarded as the only channel for fulfilling one's sexual urge. Extra- and pre-marital sexual relationships are totally forbidden and incur severe penalties in this life and in the hereafter. There is an emphasis in Islam on the prevention of social crimes rather than the creation of opportunities to commit them and Islamic law prescribes severe punishments for sex-related offences (adultery, fornication, homosexuality, rape, etc.) which are regarded as both anti-social and anti-family.

> *The adulteress and the adulterer, scourge each of them with a hundred stripes. And let not pity for them both withhold you from obedience to Allah, if you believe in Allah and the last day. Let a party of believers witness the punishment.*
>
> Al-Qur'an, chapter 24, verse 2

An objective study of the Islamic penal code will reveal that the emphasis placed on the need to maintain stability in family and community life (at the expense, if necessary, of what non-Muslims would regard as individual freedom) has the long-term benefit of deterring communal instability and has considerable wisdom.

Cleanliness (*Taharah*) is one of the basic aspects of Islam which has been likened by Prophet Muhammad (peace be upon him) to half of the faith. The Qur'an prescribes that particular attention be paid to personal cleanliness after menstruation, post-childbirth bleeding, wet dreams and intimate sexual contact, with ritual bathing being required in such instances.

The Qur'an also states that sexual relationships have the aims of procreation, physical enjoyment and achieving peace of mind; husband and wife are described as being 'garments' for each other, each to provide warmth and comfort for their partner.

> *Permitted to you, on the night of the fasts, is the approach to your wives. They are your garments and you are their garments ... associate with them, and seek what Allah has ordained for you ...*
>
> Al-Qur'an, chapter 2, verse 187

Marriage and the roles of husband and wife

> *O mankind, reverence your Guardian-Lord who created you from a single person, created, of like nature, his mate and from them both scattered (like seeds) countless men and women - fear Allah, through whom you demand your mutual rights and reverence the wombs that bore you: for Allah ever watches over you.*
>
> Al-Qur'an, chapter 4, verse 1

In Islam, marriage is the basis of family which, in turn, is the basis for a stable society. Marriage itself is a legally-binding agreement between a man and a woman which establishes their intention and mutual commitment to live together according to the teachings of the faith. They must remember their duty to Allah and to each other at all times, and that they have mutual rights and responsibilities.

The selection of marriage partners between Muslims is often regarded as old-fashioned by non-Muslims. Because Islam emphasises chastity and modesty, there is normally very little social contact between young Muslim men and women, especially of the kind which is regarded as perfectly normal in non-Muslim society. Except among 'liberal' Muslims influenced by western values who may not actually be practising Islam, there is no such thing as dating or pre-marital intimacy of any kind. In Islam, sexual behaviour and acts are only for those who are legally within the security of a marriage. There can be no sexual experimentation before marriage and fidelity within marriage is essential.

Although young people are at liberty to express their preference and state what they are looking for in a prospective partner, it is not usual practice for them to actively seek a partner for themselves. This is nearly always done by their parents, or other elders within the family. In other words, it is usually an "arranged marriage". Arranged (often misunderstood and called 'forced') marriages, highlighted in 1992 by the Scottish High Court annulment of the arranged marriage of Nasreen Akmal, should not be regarded as un-Islamic provided such marriages fulfil the basic condition of the freely-given consent of both the bride and the groom. They are the general custom amongst Muslims as the best way to find, vet and meet potential husbands or wives within the overall context of the Islamic way of life as set out above *vis-a-vis* mixing of the sexes etc. Once a potential match is arranged, the most important requirement of an Islamic marriage is the freely-given consent of the woman; without this, the marriage cannot proceed. Hence, no such situation should arise whereby women (or men, for that matter) are forced into a marriage against their wishes. Arranged marriages are not, of course, unique to Muslims; other religious groups use similar matchmaking methods and such marriages are generally more stable and less prone to divorce than so-called 'love' marriages.

Another essential condition of a marriage agreement is the *mahr* (dowry) which is paid by the man to the woman (not the reverse as in some cultures) and is for the use of the woman alone unless she decides otherwise. This can be cash, jewellery or even teaching the bride a part of the Qur'an. Payment of *mahr* is a condition of an Islamic marriage and it should be both affordable by the bridegroom and consistent with the social position of the bride who may forgo all or part of it after the marriage at her pleasure; she must not be forced to forgo it. The concept of *mahr* is at the heart of the economic freedom of women in Islam. The rate of *mahr* must not act as a disincentive to marry but those who are unable to marry should practice regular fasting until they are in a position to take this important step in life.

Islam recognises the physical and mental differences between men and women; whilst a husband and wife are companions for each other they have clearly defined roles within the family. To the husband is assigned the economic, external responsibility and leadership of the family while to the wife is assigned the management and leadership of the internal and household affairs. She should support her husband unless he asks her to disobey Allah. Conversely, the husband must be considerate towards his wife and concerned for her welfare. At all times, both husband and wife must reserve their sexuality exclusively for each other.

A Muslim woman, married or single, is a person in her own right; she is not merely an adjunct to her husband, father or brothers. Islamic Law preceded modern western law by thirteen centuries in granting women the right to own property and have their own earnings (even after marriage), something she can share with her husband or not; the decision is hers. The stereotype image of Muslim women held by many non-Muslims is that of a chattel forever in the house cooking and cleaning, with no spirituality, personality, interests or personal life; this has no basis in Islamic teachings. Islam regards men and women as completely equal in terms of accountability to Allah. However, equal doesn't mean 'the same' - physical differences and capabilities alone should demonstrate that - but both will have the same religious obligations and, if Allah wills it, the same rewards in this life or in the hereafter.

It is common for non-Muslim critics of Islam to try to 'prove' that Islam does not treat men and women equally by quoting the inheritance laws, by which men inherit a greater share of an estate than women. But if we consider the point mentioned earlier about the responsibility men have of looking after the women in their household, it should be clear that a larger inheritance helps to defray such an additional financial burden. What the women don't get as a direct legacy, they get indirectly through the inheritance of the male responsible for their upkeep.

There are many sayings of Prophet Muhammad, peace be upon him, which entreat men to show kindness and consideration for women and Muslim men must show great respect, honour and tenderness to their wives who are expected to be the mothers of their children, Allah-willing.

Within the framework of an Islamic society both men and women have the freedom to contribute to society in keeping with their own particular skills and interests, providing they do not jeopardise their personal dignity and modesty. Women are capable of handling many essential positions in society better than men (eg education - particularly primary - medicine and social work); at the time of the Prophet, peace be upon him, women played an active role in the struggle against paganism. One of the Prophet's wives, A'ishah (may Allah be pleased with her) was consulted by many people (men and women) throughout her long life as an expert on the sayings of the Prophet and Islamic jurisprudence.

The tone for the marriage relationship is set by Allah in the Qur'an:

> *And among His signs is this, that He created for you mates from among yourselves, that you may dwell in tranquillity with them and He has put love and mercy between your hearts: verily in that are signs for those who reflect.*
>
> Al-Qur'an, chapter 30, verse 21

Thus, there should be mutual respect, kindness, love, companionship and harmonious interaction between husband and wife.

Although, in practice, women generally do the domestic work in a Muslim home, this is not a legal requirement; it usually stems from the respective working roles of the husband and wife, one outside the home (usually, but not necessarily, the husband), the other within the home, looking after any children. Men should, however, help their wives in household chores, following the example of the Prophet who helped his wives and even mended his own clothes when the need arose.

In a Muslim marriage, both husband and wife have a responsibility to meet one another's sexual needs. There can be no extra-marital sexual activity for married Muslims (or, as stated earlier, pre-marital intimacy for unmarried Muslims). Adultery is not only a serious sin but also - in Islamic Law - a serious crime with severe punishments. The reason is obvious when you look at the disruption to family life and society in general as a result of adulterous behaviour.

Unlike non-Muslim marriages in the west, where pre-marital love and intimacy are considered to be almost indispensable, the basic ingredient for a successful Muslim marriage is a shared set of values upon which to build a life together. A firm shared belief in Islam can often bind couples together in their relationship which can then withstand many of the pressures which force non-Muslim couples apart.

A Muslim marriage is seen as a very real relationship between two individuals who cannot, realistically, be expected to be 100% immune from the stress and strain of everyday life. However, their shared faith will help to cushion a Muslim couple from the worst effects of such things. Nevertheless, Islam is a very practical way of life and is realistic enough to prepare couples for the possibility that they might not be able to carry on together as husband and wife, for a variety of reasons, and so divorce - although hated - is allowed when all conciliatory efforts have failed. It is essential that a marriage should be harmonious and not injurious to the life and health of the couple and their families and, ultimately, society at large.

Sexual etiquette of Islam

1. All sexual relationships must take place within the context of marriage, family life, natural modesty (*Haya'*) and morality.

2. No pre- or extra-marital sex is permitted.

3. Both husband and wife should be obedient servants of Allah; both have sexual *responsibilities*, not just avenues for pleasure, and are required to discharge such responsibilities within the bounds of His Guidance.

4. The objectives of sexual intercourse are procreation, physical pleasure, love and kindness between husband and wife.

5. Sexual relations between husband and wife must take place in private and neither party should divulge their sex-related secrets to anyone. Prophet Muhammad (peace be upon him) is reported to have said that the disclosure of sex-related secrets by either a husband or his wife *"is like a satan has met another satan on the roadside and had intercourse in full public view."* (Abu Dawud)

6. Only vaginal intercourse is allowed; anal intercourse is prohibited and severely condemned. The Prophet said, *"Do not approach women from the anus. This is like minor sodomy."* (Ahmad, Tirmidhi, Ibn Majah, Nasa'i)

7. Intercourse during menstruation and post-childbirth bleeding is not allowed. All other sexual activities - such as kissing and touching etc. - are allowed at these times. Menstruation is a biological phenomenon

which does not in itself make women unclean; they carry on with their normal routine in life with the exception of some religious duties and sexual intercourse.

8. A man must treat his wife with kindness and tenderness. Prophet Muhammad (peace be upon him) said, *"The best of you all are those who are best to their wives."* (Ibn Majah)

9. A woman should not refuse to have sexual intercourse with her husband without a reasonable excuse, as the Prophet said, *"If a man invites his wife to sleep with him and she refuses to come to him then the angels send their curses on her till the morning."* (Sahih Al-Bukhari)

10. Complete nudity between husband and wife is regarded as being against the natural instincts of modesty and decency; some covering should be used. Prophet Muhammad (peace be upon him) said, *"When anyone meets his wife, he should cover his body and they should not be naked like two camels."* (Ibn Majah)

11. Homosexuality is regarded as an abomination and is completely prohibited, there being severe punishments for homosexual acts. It is narrated by Ibn Abbas that the Prophet said, *"If you find anyone doing what the people of the time of Lut [Lot] did, then kill both the perpetrator and the perpetrated."* (Sahih Al-Bukhari and Sahih Muslim)

12. All sorts of lewdness and illicit relationships are forbidden.

13. Explicit sex-related books, films, videos etc. are prohibited.

14. A husband and wife can choose any convenient, enjoyable and satisfying position and method of intercourse except those which violate any of the guidelines (e.g. anal intercourse).

15. A full bath (*Ghusl*) is obligatory after sexual intercourse, wet dreams, menstruation and post-childbirth bleeding. Without this one cannot offer the obligatory prayers.

    And if you are in junub [state of impurity due to seminal discharge, sexual intercourse or a wet dream], *purify yourselves.*

    Al-Qur'an, chapter 5, verse 7

> *O you who believe! Do not offer your prayer ... when you are junub except when you are travelling on the road till you have taken a bath...*
>
> Al-Qur'an, chapter 4, verse 43

It is reported that the Prophet said, *"When the private part of the male touches the private part of the female, a bath is compulsory."* (Sahih Al-Bukhari, Al-Muwatta) Between acts of intercourse, or before sleeping after intercourse, it is recommended to wash the private parts and perform ablution (*wudu'*) as if for prayer. If water is unavailable or its use is dangerous to one's health, dry ablution (*Tayammum*) is allowed. One of his companions, Umar, told the Prophet, *"I became junub at night"* and he was told, *"Perform ablution, after washing your private parts, and then sleep."* In addition, when he was asked, *"May anyone of us sleep whilst in junub?"* the Prophet replied, *"Yes, if you perform ablution."* (Both Sahih Al-Bukhari)

16. Bondage, whipping, sado-masochism, masturbation*, oral sex etc. are regarded as depraved means of achieving sexual satisfaction which contradict starkly with the very purpose of sexual relationships.

17. Ibn Abbas narrates that the Prophet said, *"No man should stay with a lady in seclusion* [Khulwah] *except in the presence of a Dhu-Mahram* [a person who is legally not allowed to marry that woman]." (Sahih Al-Bukhari)

18. Intercourse should begin with a prayer (*Du'a*) by the husband and wife: *"In the name of Allah, O Allah! Protect me from the satan and protect what you bestow upon us* [ie a child] *from satan."* (Sahih Al-Bukhari)

19. Parents should not be shy about providing necessary information on sexual matters to their children. This will discourage them from receiving and believing unwholesome and inaccurate information from their peers.

20. Any kind of dress which is likely to arouse sexual passions is discouraged. When going out and meeting people with whom marriage is possible (*Ghair Mahram* - according to Islamic Law), women should wear modest

---

*The majority of Islamic jurists consider that masturbation is prohibited (*Haram*). Imam Ahmad Ibn Hanbal and Ibn Hazm permit it in two circumstances: i. If there is a fear of committing adultery (Zina) if sexual relief is not otherwise obtained, and ii. if there is a financial inability to marry. The Prophet (peace be upon him) advised young Muslims unable to marry to practise frequent fasting as this develops will-power, self-control and the fear of Allah. (*Fiqhus Sunnah*, volume 2)

dress (Hijab), covering the whole body (except the face and hands) in such a way and with such material that does not show the contours of the body, either by being too tight or by being transparent.

Tell the believing men to lower their gaze and guard their private parts. That is purer for them. Surely Allah knows what you do. And tell the believing women to lower their gaze and guard their private parts and not to display their beauty except what is apparent, to draw their cloaks over their bosom and not to reveal their feminine beauty except to their husbands or fathers or their husband's father or their sons or their husband's sons or their brothers or their brothers' sons or their sisters' sons or their women or their maids or impotent male attendants or children who do not know of women's private parts. And let them not walk noisily so as to reveal what they preserve of their beauty. And turn to Allah together, O believers, in order that you may prosper.

Al-Qur'an, chapter 24, verses 30-31

21. *'Awrah* refers to those parts of the body which modesty requires to be covered. For males, the *'awrah* is that part of the body between the navel and the knees; for females, it is the whole body except the face and hands. A man is not allowed to bare his *'awrah* before anyone except his wife and *vice versa*. In addition, a woman may not show any part of her body from the chest to the knees to males whom she cannot marry (eg her father, brother, son, uncle, nephew etc.). In other words, she can go without a headcovering or with a sleeveless garment, for example, in front of these men if she wishes. Further, she should not show any part of her body between the navel and the knees to any Muslim female, nor any part of her *'awrah* at all to any non-Muslim female.

Promiscuity, sexually transmitted diseases and AIDS

Promiscuity, both heterosexual and homosexual, leads to innumerable problems in society: for an Islamic society, based as it is on family life, trust, fidelity, love and accountability to Allah, promiscuous behaviour based solely on selfish physical gratification with little care for the ultimate consequences of one's actions is totally unacceptable. Apart from the break-ups of family relationships (with the resultant proliferation of single-parent families and the psychological effects on adults and children alike) such behaviour spreads both physical and mental disease, the most serious of which is AIDS.

Of course, a cure must be found (insha'Allah - Allah willing) to help those unfortunate to have AIDS or who are HIV positive, that is, they have the virus which could develop into 'full-blown' AIDS. Such efforts are a humanitarian necessity. However, while the scientists are trying to make the breakthrough in their search for a cure, Islam has some very positive and radical things to say about how the disease is caught and spread in the first place.

> Prophet Muhammad said, "Every intoxicant is khamr and every khamr is haram [forbidden]."
>
> Sahih Muslim

> *Let those who find not the wherewithal for marriage keep themselves chaste...*
>
> Al-Qur'an, chapter 24, verse 33

> *...do you commit lewdness such as no people in creation (ever) committed before you? For you practise your lusts on men in preference to women: you are indeed a people transgressing beyond bounds.*
>
> Al-Qur'an chapter 7, verse 81

All of the means by which AIDS is transmitted - drug abuse, sexual promiscuity and homosexual acts - are forbidden in Islam. Clearly, this puts Muslims in a minority (or so the media would have us believe) because such acts are considered to be acceptable in society today. Anyone who declares that homosexuality is a perverted way of life - as Muslims must - is accused of intolerance. Muslims believe, though, that such behaviour has been forbidden by Allah (God) for very real reasons and if we ignore His guidance there are bound to be harmful effects on society. The undeniable facts show that male homosexual activity is the most common cause of the AIDS virus spreading in the west: of the 5,894 cases of AIDS in Britain reported between January 1982 and April 1992, 78% were homosexual men. Only 8.6% were due to heterosexual transmission and less than 1% were between couples in this country (ie not contracted overseas) without known risk factors such as drug use etc. (Source: *Communicable Disease Report*, Vol. 2, No. 21, May 1992) Islam prohibited anal intercourse of any kind, even between husband and wife, over fourteen hundred years ago!

Muslims believe that sex education which does not actively discourage sexua experimentation before marriage should be stopped. The advice usually offere to people (especially young people) in the efforts to prevent AIDS withou "spoiling sexual enjoyment" frequently overlooks the doubtful advisability an morality of casual sexual liaisons. Instead of assuming that because some people are sexually active at a young age all young people must be given as much information and contraceptive advice as possible, more attention should be paid to getting the message across that "No sex before marriage" is the most effective form of contraception and the "safest sex" of all.

The concept of what constitutes "acceptable" behaviour in society needs to be redefined. It is often said that if you want to know the future, look into the past: history shows that the major civilisations all collapsed once homosexuality was accepted as normal behaviour. Sadly, in this very secular world, the guidance given by Allah is rejected more often than not. It is shocking for Muslim parents to read that "Only 3 per cent of young people [aged 16-24] believe that sexual intercourse should be reserved for marriage, with nearly half admitting to their first experience before the age of 16..." (*The Independent*, 21 July 1992)

Muslims believe that Islam has the answers for the problems of life and should be listened to for the benefit of everyone. A stable, lasting, responsible and caring society is only possible where sexual relationships are based on heterosexual marriage with neither the scope nor the need for extra-marital affairs and deviant practices such as homosexuality.

Contraception

Sex education invariably includes a study of contraceptive devices and methods. Contraception is seen by many as being the best way to allow young people to experiment with sexuality without the fear of unwanted pregnancy: *'Limit the damage and increase the enjoyment'* is one way that this concept has been described. Although contraception is often called 'planned parenthood', attempts to enforce it in Third World countries contain the hallmarks of population control by the 'developed world'.

Islam limits the permitted use of contraception. In a society where extra- and pre-marital sex is forbidden and there is no free-mixing between adult men and women it closes all avenues which lead to the need for contraception. However, it is allowed on the following grounds:

i. If there is a danger to the life of the mother if she gets pregnant.
ii. If there is a fear of resorting to forbidden acts to earn sufficient money to maintain a large family.
iii. If there is fear for the baby's health if a nursing mother becomes pregnant (*Ghilah*).

Imam Ahmad Ibn Hanbal is of the opinion that the consent of the wife is essential before any contraception is used because she has a right both to sexual enjoyment and to decide whether or not she wants a child. Using contraceptive devices because you fear poverty if a child is born is forbidden as this contradicts the belief that Allah is the Sustainer of and Provider for all creatures.

Abortion

Whilst Islam permits certain forms of contraception for specific valid reasons, the violation of a pregnancy once it has commenced is not allowed except in the circumstances mentioned below.

Muslim scholars agree that abortion is forbidden; it is a crime against a live human being. Such is the crime that if an aborted baby is alive when removed from its mother's womb and subsequently dies, blood money is payable. If the baby is aborted dead, then a smaller amount of blood money becomes due.

If, though, it is reliably established (by a Muslim doctor with detailed knowledge of Islamic Law on the subject) that the continuation of the pregnancy will result in the death of the mother, then the principle of choosing the lesser of two evils is followed, and an abortion is allowable. The mother's life takes precedence over that of her baby in such an instance because the mother is already established in life with many duties and responsibilities. It is less disruptive to family life (although just as regrettable) to thus sacrifice the life of the unborn child which has not yet acquired a personality nor has any duties, responsibilities or obligations.

Imam Al-Ghazzali (born 1058, died 1111) distinguished between contraception and abortion by saying, "Contraception is not like abortion. Abortion is a crime against an existing being. Existence has various stages. The first is the settling of the semen in the womb and its mixing with the secretions [egg] of the woman. It is then ready to receive life. Disturbing it is a crime. When it develops further and becomes a lump, abortion is a greater crime. When it acquires a soul and its creation is complete the crime becomes even more grievous. The crime reaches its maximum seriousness after the foetus is separated from its mother alive." (Al-Ihya, book of Al-Nikah [Marriage], p.74)

In Arabia before the advent of Islam the tribal custom was to bury unwanted baby girls alive. This abominable practice was prohibited and there are two verses of the Qur'an connected with that which could also be applied directly to the circumstances of abortion:

> *...do not slay your children because of poverty - We provide for you and for them...*
>
> Al-Qur'an, chapter 6, verse 151

> *Slay not your children, fearing a fall to poverty. We shall provide*

for them and for you. Lo! the slaying of them is a great sin
Al-Qur'an, chapter 17, verse 31

Those who advocate the belief that abortion is permissible because "a woman has the right to decide what she does with her own body" should consider the following: Did they decide for themselves when they were to be born? No. Do they decide for themselves when they are going to die? No. Did they decide for themselves when they became pregnant in the first place? No. Did they decide for themselves to have intercourse with the possibility of having an unwanted child? In most cases, yes. That is the time when a woman has a right to choose, not after life has begun in her womb, a life which in itself has a right to exist and grow.

Sex Education in Schools

Allah has made natural arrangements for humans to learn about their sexuality as they grow and develop but young people are in need of factual knowledge to cope with real-life situations. Hence, in Islam we are provided with specific information about menstruation, childbirth and marriage. There are also clear guidelines on sexual etiquette within lawful marriage. Any sexual activity outside marriage is forbidden.

> *They question you (O Muhammad) concerning menstruation. Say, it is an illness, so let women alone at such times and go not unto them till they are cleansed and when they have purified themselves, then go in unto them as Allah has enjoined upon you. No doubt, Allah loves those who turn unto Him and loves those who have a care for cleanliness.*
>
> Al-Qur'an, chapter 2, verse 222

> *O Mankind! If you have a doubt about the resurrection, (consider) that We created you out of dust, then out of sperm, then out of a leech-like clot, then out of a morsel of flesh, partly formed and partly unformed...*
>
> Al-Qur'an, chapter 22, verse 5

> *Prohibited to you (for marriage) are - your mothers, daughters, sisters; father's sisters, mother's sisters, brother's daughters, sister's daughters; foster-mothers (who suckled you), foster-sisters; your wives' mothers; your step-daughters under your guardianship, born of your wives to whom you have gone in - no prohibition if you have not gone in - (Those who have been) wives of your sons proceeding from your loins; and two sisters in wedlock at one and the same time...*
>
> Al-Qur'an, chapter 4, verse 23

> *And approach not fornication; surely it is shameful and an evil, opening the road (to other evils).*
>
> Al-Qur'an, chapter 17, verse 32

Since there may be many sceptics who doubt the validity of using text from the Qur'an as a teaching aid in sex education it may be worthwhile to know that the word *'alaq*, which is most often translated as "a clot of blood" or, as in the example above, "a leech-like clot", contains within it the meaning that this is "something which clings". It is now known, 1400+ years after the revelation of the Qur'an, that the fertilised egg literally *clings* to the wall of the womb!

Although parents usually find it difficult to talk about sex with their children (and surveys have shown that parents shy away from this), in our opinion they are the right people to deal with this delicate and important topic. However, the law thinks otherwise and so sex education is on the curriculum in every school unless the governors decide otherwise, as is their right under the Education (No 2) Act 1986 (The 1986 Act), section 18 (2)(a)(b). It is probably fair to say that the majority of Muslim parents would be happier if there was no sex education in schools at all. Since this is unrealistic in today's social climate, Muslims must look for ways to safeguard their children from the undesirable effects of liberal sex education. Those who are keen to practise their religion in this country must work towards full recognition of their religious requirements by the government, and sex education must be included on the agenda.

In Islam, marriage is the only basis for family life and sexual relationships, in sharp contrast to society at large wherein extra-marital sex is not only tolerated but is also almost the norm. Muslims feel strongly, therefore, that any sex education in schools is given "...with due regard to moral considerations and the value of family life." (The 1986 Act, Section 46) To ensure that this is the case, Muslim parents must make every effort to contact their children's schools and ask for full information on the contents of the sex education programme. If there is anything objectionable in use, parents should make their objections known to the board of governors who have a duty under section 18 (3)(a)(i) of the 1986 Act to have regard "to any representations which are made to them, with regard to any of those matters [ie sex education], by any persons connected with the community served by the school." In Circular 11/87 issued by the then Department of Education & Science (now the Department for Education) it was stated that whilst parents have no statutory right to withdraw children from sex education lessons, governors will have the non-statutory "discretion to accept or reject requests from parents for their children to be withdrawn from any sex education to which they object." Subsequent changes to include some sex education concerning HIV and AIDS in the National Curriculum mean, of course, that there can be no withdrawal whatsoever from those particular parts of the sex education programme.

Parents should be aware that some of the material prepared for sex education lessons is produced by outside agencies who have an agenda far removed from the sort of concerns Muslims have for their children. Anything produced by bodies such as Brook Advisory Centres and the Family Planning Association, for example, must be scrutinised in detail by Muslim parents before they agree to it being given or shown to their children because the underlying philosophy of these organisations is at odds with Islamic teaching. For example, the Brook publication *Safe Sex for Teenagers* (1978) states: "We must be prepared to challenge our established attitudes that sexual activity in young people is dangerous." Islam has no qualms about young people being sexually active *within marriage* but the Brook concept revolves around the fact that such youngsters are unlikely to be married. Both Brook and the FPA erroneously assume that a) all teenagers are having sexual intercourse and, b) those who aren't will do so at any moment and so all must have contraceptive protection.

Muslims believe that pupils should be informed that no contraceptive method - *apart from abstinence* - is 100% safe (eg they should be told that out of 733 women who had abortions in one British city between September 1988 and March 1989, 334 reported that their partners used condoms for contraceptive 'protection' [Source: *The British Journal of Family Planning*, 1990, 15:112-117]); that there are dangerous side-effects to 'The Pill'; that venereal diseases are dangerous and that abortion is forbidden except in exceptional circumstances. Details of the emotional effects of early sexual intercourse should also be prominent in sex education; without pointing out that young people expose themselves to intolerable stress by unbridled sexual experimentation it is likely to do more long-term harm than good. Muslim parents must be conscious of these factors.

In our view, sex education should not be treated just as another academic subject leading to examination and assessment; it should form part of Personal and Social Education, Health and Hygiene and/or Biology lessons. Where possible, single-sex lessons should be arranged, especially on matters such as contraception and suchlike, as this will ensure the confident participation of girls, something which is not always forthcoming in mixed-sex classes.

Information about the bodily changes involved in growing up should be set out for children objectively (and within the context of the 1986 Act), paying full attention to the moral and religious dimensions. It is to be regretted that much of the mechanics of sex, including contraceptive devices, are explored in depth whilst the emotional and spiritual impact such details can have on some children is all too often ignored.

It appears that those responsible for sex education make no allowances for the fact that children develop physically *and* psychologically at different ages. Children should only be given potentially disturbing information when they and their parents feel they are ready to receive it in the right frame of mind instead of the present situation whereby sex education is given to all children at a certain age, regardless of their mental readiness. Provision of information on sex and growth etc. to children at a very early age (say, at 7 years old) is sometimes counter-productive.

Goodwill and understanding is essential if problems are to be resolved in a manner acceptable to all and there should be an amicable way of looking at the problems caused by sex education. Preconceived ideas and a lack of knowledge producing ill-founded fears should not be used as excuses for closing the doors of consultation. Long-cherished beliefs and values, including equality for all citizens, should make for sensitivity to the difficulties faced by Muslims in all aspects of life, including sex education.

Having said that, the basic responsibility for passing faith and heritage to young children rests largely with parents, who should set a good example for their children. If this is not done, parents should not expect them to live up to their own ideals and values. Young Muslims must deal with a multi-cultural society and try to carve their own niche outside the home. If parents set them good examples then it is reasonable to expect that they will try to emulate their elders and, in turn, set a good example for their own children in the future.

Muslim organisations also have a responsibility to help young Muslims grow with a healthy Islamic identity. Combined effort from parents and organisations is essential if the community is to combat the undesirable influences of a secular society.

Appendix I

The following is the complete text of Circular number 11/87 issued by what was the Department of Education and Science (now called the Department for Education) on the 25 September 1987 to "All Local Education Authorities" (sections in bold have been highlighted by the author of this book, not the DES):

"DES Circular No. 11/87"

Sex Education at School

Introduction

1. Appropriate and responsible sex education is an important element in the work of schools in preparing pupils for adult life. It calls for careful and sensitive treatment.

2. Parents are the key figures in helping their children cope with the physical and emotional aspects of growing up and in preparing them for the challenges and responsibilities which sexual maturity brings. The teaching offered by schools should be complementary and supportive to the role of parents. But some parents may not feel able to discuss sexual matters fully and freely with their children. Because of this schools have a clear responsibility to ensure that pupils are adequately prepared for adult life.

3. This circular is set within the general context of new statutory provisions relating to the school curriculum contained in the Education (No 2) Act 1986. The Secretary of State has now initiated wide consultations on the Government's proposals for legislation on the national curriculum which will affect these provisions and responsibilities for the curriculum within schools. The 1986 Act places responsibility on governing bodies for determining what sex education should be offered in their schools and the Secretary of State believes that LEAs and governing bodies will welcome guidance on the effect of the new framework for the provision of sex education established by the 1986 Act and on other aspects of the treatment of sexual matters within the school context. This Circular is concerned mainly with the compulsory period of schooling from age 5 to 16; but many of the considerations will have implications also for provision for pupils above that age range. It should be read in conjunction with the guidance in DES circulars 6/86 and 7/87 on other provisions of the 1986 Act.

Control over the Content and Organisation of Sex Education

4. For county, controlled and maintained special schools, section 18(2) of the Education (No 2) Act 1986 requires that:

> "The articles of government for every such school shall provide for it to be the duty of the governing body:
>
> a. to consider separately (while having regard to the local education authority's statement under section 17 of this Act [on their policy in relation to the secular curriculum in maintained schools]) the question whether sex education should form part of the secular curriculum for the school; and
>
> b. to make, and keep up to date, a separate written statement:
>
> i. of their policy with regard to the content and organisation of the relevant part of the curriculum; or
>
> ii. where they conclude that sex education should not form part of the secular curriculum, of that conclusion."

Section 18(6) requires that:

> "The articles of government for every such school shall provide for it to be the duty of the head teacher, in discharging his duties in relation to the secular curriculum for the school:
>
> c. to ensure that the curriculum:
>
> i. so far as it relates to sex education, is compatible with the governing body's policy (as expressed in their statement ...) except where that policy is incompatible with any part of the syllabus for a course which forms part of that curriculum and leads to a public examination."

These provisions will take effect progressively from 1 September 1987 as new articles of government under the 1986 Act are made. The articles of government for all such schools newly established after 1 September 1987 must satisfy the above requirements. The articles of existing county and maintained special schools must comply with these requirements by 1 September 1988, or such earlier date on which new articles or a new instrument of government are made for the school. For voluntary controlled schools the final date is 1 September 1989.

5. For all voluntary aided and special agreement schools, section 19(1) of the Act requires the articles of government to provide inter alia for the content of the secular curriculum to be under the control of the governing body; for the governing body to have regard to the policy of the local education authority as to the curriculum for the authority's schools; and for the head teacher to be allocated by the governing body such functions as will, subject to the resources available, enable him to determine and organise the curriculum. Articles of government for aided and special agreement schools newly established after 1 September 1987 must satisfy the above requirements. The articles of existing schools must comply with these requirements by 1 September 1989 or such earlier date on which new articles or a new instrument of government for the school is made. Section 18 of the Act does not apply to these schools, and section 19 makes no separate provision for sex education as compared with other parts of the secular curriculum. Nevertheless, the Secretary of State hopes that in discharging their responsibilities, the governing bodies and head teachers of these schools will as far as possible have due regard to the general guidance of this circular.

The Role of Governors

6. In determining their policy for sex education, governors will also be required under the Act to have regard to any representations made to them by any persons connected with the community served by the school and to any representations made by the chief officer of police connected with his responsibilities. In the case of county, controlled and maintained special schools the governors will be statutorily required to consult the head teacher. The Secretary of State expects that governors will find useful the professional advice which the head and other staff are able to offer and the experience and expertise of teacher representatives on the governing body. The governors will also find it helpful to take account of the references to sex education in the HMI discussion document "Health Education from 5-16" (Curriculum Matters 6, HMSO 1986). Ultimately the content of the policy will be for the governors to decide, subject to the requirements of section 46 of the 1986 Act that sex education should be given in such a manner as to encourage pupils to have due regard to moral considerations and the value of family life (see paragraph 18 below). Whilst it may be some time for some schools before the requirements of sections 18 and 19 of the 1986 Act take effect,

all governing bodies may well wish to consider what their policy on sex education will be before the sections take effect.

7. Section 18(2)(a) of the Act allows a governing body to decide that no sex education should be provided in their school. However, the Secretary of State expects that, in exercising their new powers, governing bodies will be strongly influenced by the widely-accepted view, that schools have a responsibility to their pupils to offer at least some education about sexual matters. In particular, pupils may need to know about sexual matters to ensure that education about health is not impaired, and that, for example, they understand about the relationship between certain forms of sexual behaviour and AIDS (see paragraph 23 below).

8. The Secretary of State envisages that governors, as part of their responsibility for deciding policy on the content of any sex education to be offered may determine their school's overall approach to teaching about sexual matters. They should consider whether and how parents should be given opportunities to see teaching materials for themselves and to receive explanations of the way in which they are to be used. They should also have a policy on whether and how to use outside speakers on particular topics, whose contributions would need to be consistent with both the governors' overall policy for sex education and with statutory requirements. But the governors should maintain a distinction between their responsibility for determining general policy on content and organisation, and the exercise of professional skills by the head teacher and staff in delivering the curriculum in accordance with the policy.

9. As part of their responsibility for determining policy on the organisation of sex education provision, the governors may wish to consider the extent to which it should form a discrete element in the curriculum or be spread across different programmes. They will also have the discretion to accept or reject requests from parents for their children to be withdrawn from any sex education to which they object. There is no statutory right for parents to cause their children to be withdrawn from sex education provision. However, some parents will have strong objections on religious grounds to their children receiving sex education and governing bodies should fully appreciate this in exercising their discretion.

The Role of Parents

10. **The increased proportion of elected parent representatives on governing bodies, provided for under the 1986 Act, will ensure that due weight is given to parental views in formulating the sex education policy for the**

school. Parents will also have the following opportunities, provided under statute, to be more closely involved in these and other aspects of their children's schooling.

11. The Education (School Information) Regulations 1981, made under Section 8 of the Education Act 1980, already require **local education authorities and governors of aided and special agreement schools to publish information about "the manner and context in which education as respects sexual matters is given".** The information will in future need to refer to the governors' policy on content and organisation, to any arrangements for parental consultation over the type of materials to be used, and to any discretionary arrangements for excusing pupils from sex education. With effect from 7 January 1987, the governing body of every county, voluntary and maintained special school has been required to publish an annual report for parents on the work of the school. That report and any other matters of interest to parents will be for discussion at an annual meeting of the full parent body, which will be able to pass formal resolutions which the governing body, the head teacher or the local education authority will be obliged to consider. Any concerns about the school's approach to sex education may thus be raised in this forum.

The Role of the Head

12. In discharging their responsibilities for the curriculum, including securing its delivery, the head teachers of county, controlled or maintained special schools will under the 1986 Act be bound by the governing body's stated policy, except where that policy is incompatible with any part of the syllabus for a course within the curriculum leading to a public examination. Where, for example, the syllabus for such a course in biology requires that pupils demonstrate some understanding of the facts relating to family planning, teaching in accordance with that syllabus is permitted, notwithstanding any indication to the contrary in the governing body's policy statement on sex education. With the help of the teaching staff, the head will have an important part to play in contributing to the preparation, and keeping up to date, of the policy statement. In exercising all these responsibilities, the head teacher of such a school is also bound by the requirement of section 46 of the 1986 Act (see paragraph 18 below).

The Role of Teachers

13. The Secretary of State considers that the majority of the teachers involved have hitherto fulfilled their responsibilities in relation to this aspect of the

curriculum with skill and sensitivity. The effective discharge of their responsibilities in implementing the governors' policy at classroom level will depend in large measure on their professional skill and expertise, possibly making use of the expertise of health service professionals.

The Role of the LEA

14. Section 17 of the 1986 Act requires LEAs to determine their policies in respect of the secular curriculum for county, controlled and maintained special schools, having considered the range and internal balance of that curriculum. In carrying out that duty, LEAs will need to decide to what extent their policy statements, which will be subject to section 46 of the Act, should refer specifically to sex education. The governors will be obliged to have regard to the relevant parts of the LEA's statement, but will not be bound by them.

The Place of Sex Education within the 5-16 Curriculum

15. At the primary level particular care and sensitivity is needed in matching teaching to the maturity of the pupils involved, which may not always be adequately indicated by chronological age. At this level, teaching should aim to help pupils cope with the physical and emotional challenges of growing up and give them an elementary understanding of human reproduction. **Pupils' questions should be answered sensitively and with due consideration for any particular religious or cultural factors bearing on the discussion of sexual issues.**

16. In the secondary phase, sex education does not usually feature as a discrete subject on the timetable but is commonly subsumed within a broader programme of personal and social education or health education. Whilst the physical aspects of sexual behaviour may well be encompassed within the teaching of biology, opportunities for considering the broader emotional and ethical dimensions of sexual attitudes and mores may arise with other subject areas.

Teaching in Special Schools

17. Special schools have a particularly sensitive role to play. Although all parents have had to cope with the problems of their own puberty and sexual development, very few of them are themselves disabled in any way and may have difficulty in understanding the extra problems of the disabled. Children with learning difficulties need more help than others in coping with the physical and

emotional stresses of growing up; they also need more help in learning what sorts of behaviour are and are not acceptable, and they may need to be warned and prepared against unacceptable behaviour by adults. On the other hand some parents may find it difficult to come to terms with the idea that disabled children will some day become sexually active. The governors of special schools - and of any schools which cater for pupils with special educational needs - will need to take particular care in working out their policy, and in ensuring that the support of parents is enlisted in implementing it.

A Moral Framework for Sex Education

18. Section 46 of the Education (No 2) Act 1986 requires that:

> "The local education authority by whom any county, voluntary or special school is maintained, and the governing body and head teacher of the school, shall take such steps as are reasonably practicable to secure that where sex education is given to any registered pupils at the school it is given in such a manner as to encourage those pupils to have due regard to moral considerations and the value of family life."

Section 46 came into force on 7 January 1987, and the duty is imposed on all the parties specified.

19. The Secretary of State considers that the aims of a programme of sex education should be to present facts in an objective and balanced manner so as to enable pupils to comprehend the range of sexual attitudes and behaviour in present day society; to know what is and is not legal; to consider their own attitudes, and to make informed, reasoned and responsible decisions about the attitudes which they will adopt both while they are at school and in adulthood. Teaching about the physical aspects of sexual behaviour should be set within a clear moral framework in which pupils are encouraged to consider the importance of self-restraint, dignity and respect for themselves and others, and helped to recognise the physical, emotional and moral risks of casual and promiscuous sexual behaviour. Schools should foster a recognition that both sexes should behave responsibly in sexual matters. Pupils should be helped to appreciate the benefits of stable married and family life and the responsibilities of parenthood.

20. Schools have a responsibility to ensure that pupils understand those aspects of the law which relate to sexual activity. Pupils should understand three things in particular, which are that:

i. except in certain very restricted circumstances, it is a criminal offence for a man or boy to have sexual intercourse with a girl under 16, irrespective of whether she consents;

ii. homosexual acts (defined as buggery or gross indecency) between males constitute a criminal offence unless both parties have attained the age of 21 and the acts are committed with the consent of both in private (ie where only the two parties are present); and

iii. it is an offence to make an indecent assault on a person; and a girl or boy under 16 cannot in law give any consent which would prevent an act being an assault for the purpose of this offence.

21. Schools cannot, in general, avoid tackling controversial sexual matters, such as contraception and abortion, by reason of their sensitivity. Pupils may well ask questions about them and schools should be prepared to offer balanced and factual information and to acknowledge the major ethical issues involved. Where schools are founded on specific religious principles this will have a direct bearing on the manner in which such subjects are presented.

22. There is no place in any school in any circumstances for teaching which advocates homosexual behaviour, which presents it as the "norm", or which encourages homosexual experimentation by pupils. Indeed, encouraging or procuring homosexual acts by pupils who are under the age of consent is a criminal offence. It must also be recognised that for many people, including members of various religious faiths, homosexual practice is not morally acceptable, and deep offence may be caused to them if the subject is not handled with sensitivity by teachers if discussed in the classroom.

Teaching about AIDS

23. The Government has emphasised that the key to limiting the spread of AIDS lies in enhanced public understanding about the disease and the ways in which infection is and is not transmitted. Schools can contribute towards the general level of awareness through the teaching which they offer. The Secretary of State believes that education about AIDS is an important element in the teaching programmes offered to pupils in the later years of compulsory schooling. Schools should also be prepared to respond to questions about AIDS from younger pupils. Schools have a clear responsibility to warn pupils of the health risks of casual and promiscuous sexual behaviour - whether heterosexual or

homosexual - and of the dangers of drug abuse. Whatever the overall policy on sex education adopted by the governing body, particular attention should be given to the forms of sexual and other behaviour which carry a risk of infection with the AIDS virus and about ways in which risks may be avoided or lessened.

24. So that teachers and other education service professionals may themselves be fully and accurately informed about AIDS, the Department has issued (together with the Welsh, Scottish and Northern Ireland Offices) a factual booklet ["AIDS : Some Questions and Answers" (1987)] to staff in all schools. The Secretary of State has announced the commissioning of a video package for use with pupils in the later secondary years, which will be made available to schools shortly, and the need for teaching materials is under review. The DES/Welsh Office booklet "Children at School and Problems related to AIDS" (issued in 1986) gave advice on measures to be taken in schools to avoid the spread of infection and to care for infected pupils.

Advice to Pupils under 16

25. It is important to distinguish between, on the one hand, the school's function of providing education generally about sexual matters on the basis described above and, on the other, counselling and advice to individual pupils particularly if this relates to their own sexual behaviour. Good teachers have always taken a pastoral interest in the welfare and well-being of pupils. But this function should never trespass on the proper exercise of parental rights and responsibilities.

26. On the specific question of the provision of contraceptive advice to girls under 16, the general rule must be that giving an individual pupil advice on such matters without parental knowledge or consent would be an inappropriate exercise of a teacher's professional responsibilities, and could, depending on the circumstances, amount to a criminal offence. The provision of contraceptive advice and treatment was addressed by the House of Lords judgement in the Gillick case[1]. The House of Lords found that, while it should be most unusual for a doctor to provide such a service to a child under 16 without parental knowledge or consent, there were circumstances, described in the judgements, where he or she would be justified in doing so. These circumstances hinged essentially upon the nature and context of medical advice and treatment in connection with the supply and use of contraceptive devices. They have no parallel in school education.

27. A teacher approached by a pupil for advice on these or other aspects of sexual behaviour should, wherever possible, encourage the pupil to seek advice from his or her parents. Where the circumstances are such as to lead the teacher to believe that the pupil has embarked upon, or is contemplating, a course of conduct which is likely to place him or her in moral or physical danger, or in breach of the law, the teacher has a general duty to warn the pupil of the risks involved. Whether the teacher should take the matter further, by informing the head teacher, and whether the head teacher should consider involving the pupil's parents, the specialist support services, or the local education authority, will depend on the particular circumstances involved and the professional judgement of the staff.

28. Guidance on the action to be taken in cases of suspected child abuse and the role of schools in educating children about the dangers, will be the subject of a separate circular later this year.

Action.

29. Action should be taken in accordance with sections 17-19 of the Education (No 2) Act 1986 by:

a. local education authorities, to consider the place of sex education in their statements of policy on the secular curriculum for their schools (paragraph 14 of this circular), and the appropriate support for those involved in giving sex education (paragraph 13);

b. governing bodies of county, controlled and maintained special schools, to prepare and keep up to date, their statements of policy on the content and organisation of any sex education in their schools (paragraphs 4-9). Whilst this requirement will take effect over a period of time for all schools, governing bodies may wish to begin to prepare their policy before being required to do so by the law;

c. governing bodies of aided and special agreement schools, as their revised articles of government come into effect, to determine the content of the secular curriculum, having regard to the policy of the local education authority as to the curriculum for the authority's schools;

d. head teachers and their staff, to plan and carry out programmes of sex education in accordance with the governors' policy (paragraphs 12-13);

e. all the above parties, to perform their respective functions in accordance with section 46 of the Act and in the light of the guidance in this circular (paragraphs 15-29).

Enquiries

30. All enquiries relating to this circular should be addressed in the first instance to:

Mr. T P Dracup, Rm 4/91, Schools Branch 3, Department of Education and Science, York Road, London, SE1 7PH.

D J S Hancock

1. Gillick v. West Norfolk and Wisbech Area Health Authority and the Department of Health and Social Security [1986] AC 112

NB Any queries on the above should now, of course, be addressed to Schools Branch 3, Department for Education, Sanctuary Buildings, Great Smith Street, London, SW1P 3BT. Telephone 071 925 5000.

Appendix II

Open Letter to Muslim Parents

Dear brothers and sisters in Islam,

Assalamu Alaikum wa Rahmatullahi wa Barakatuh.

Now more than ever before it is vital for you to take an active interest in the sort of sex education which is being offered to your children in their schools. There are things you can do to make life easier for your children and their teachers; all it needs is a little effort on your part.

It is important that you should:

1. Know the law regarding sex education (see Appendix 1).

2. Know what actually goes on in your children's school in the name of sex education.

3. Ask the head teacher, in writing, to provide you with full details of the sex education curriculum, including a time when you can see for yourself the materials, books, tapes etc. used. (A sample letter you could use follows this letter for your assistance.)

4. Write to the school governors and ask that they excuse your children from sex education if you feel that what is taught is against Islamic teachings on the subject. At the same time, take the opportunity to inform the governors of the Islamic viewpoint on sex education; if you can inform the head teacher and the local education authority as well, so much the better.

5. Talk to the other Muslim parents at your children's school and make a united approach to the school on this subject. We would suggest that you form a 'Muslim Parents Association' which can also deal with the school on other important issues of concern.

6. Make sure that whatever else happens, you actually talk to your children as they grow up and provide them with knowledge of human biological development within an Islamic context. Use this booklet as a guide.

7. Keep in touch with your local mosque and Muslim organisations so that issues such as sex education may be dealt with on a wider scale and all parents can be kept up to date with developments affecting schools and your children.

8. Take every opportunity to organise or attend public meetings on sex education so that parents can be made aware of the objectionable material used in schools. If possible, liaise with non-Muslim organisations (such as Family and Youth concern, for example) which have similar aims and objectives in this respect.

Remember that it is your responsibility to give your children the best possible start in life so that they are not fed distorted information which erodes the Islamic values we all hold so dear.

May Allah, subhanahu wa ta'ala guide us all in this important matter. Amin.

Wassalamu Alaikum.

Sample letter for use by parents

The following letter is based on a questionnaire compiled by a head of department of a London comprehensive school. You should copy it and send it to the head teacher of your children's school.

(The letter was originally in *Sex Education: it's uses and abuses*, published by the Responsible Society, now known as Family and Youth Concern)

Dear Head teacher,

Re: Sex education in your school

I would be grateful if you could give me the following details regarding the above subject:

a. The aim and purpose of sex education in the school.
b. Who is responsible for the sex education - form teachers, subject teachers, specialist teachers or outside agencies?

c. Is sex education placed within the overall syllabus of any particular department - science, religious education, social studies, humanities - or does it receive separate treatment?

d. What is the content of sex education in terms of:
   1. moral teachings
   2. social setting
   3. biological facts
   4. medical information of any other kind?

e. At what age do pupils receive sex education?

f. What visual or audio aids (films, slides, tapes etc.) are used? What are the titles, content and by whom are they produced?

g. What books are used? Who are the authors and publishers?

h. Is there any other literature used? If so, what are the titles and the names of the authors and publishers?

i. Are any outside agencies or speakers involved at any time? If so, what is their purpose, are they supervised by school staff while with the children, how long do they spend with the pupils and with pupils of what age do they deal?

j. What is the policy of your school for notifying parents of the content and methodology of sex education and for inviting their comments and/or participation?

k. What arrangements are made for parents to view any material used in sex education lessons?

l. What arrangements are there for parents to withdraw their children from sex education if they so wish?

I look forward to hearing from you as a matter of urgency.

Yours faithfully,

(Parent/Guardian of [name of pupil/s])

Appendix III

Select Bibliography

1. *The Holy Qur'an: text, translation and commentary*, Abdullah Yusuf Ali, Amana Corporation, USA.
2. *The Glorious Qur'an*, translation by Muhammad Marmaduke Pickthall, Taj Co. Ltd., Karachi, 1975.
3. *Tafhimul Qur'an* (Urdu, vol. III), Abul 'Ala Mawdudi, Lahore, 1975.
4. *The Qur'an: Basic Teachings*, Irving, Ahmad and Ahsan, The Islamic Foundation, Leicester, 1979.
5. Study of the Qur'an, lessons 1-19, Al-Qur'an Society, London.
6. *Sahih Al-Bukhari* (vols. I & VII), English translation by Dr. M. Muhsin Khan, 1973.
7. *Al-Muwatta of Imam Malik*, English translation by A.A. Tarjumana & Yaqub Johnson, Diwan Press, 1982.
8. *The Lawful and the Prohibited in Islam*, Yusuf Al-Qaradawi, American Trust Publications, USA.
9. *Sexuality in Islam*, Abdul Wahab Bouhdiba, Routledge & Keegan Paul, 1985.
10. *School Sex Education: Why, What and How?*, Doreen E. Massey, Family Planning Association, 1988.
11. *Some Notes on Sex Education*, London County Council, 1964.
12. *Sex Education: Its Uses and Abuses*, K. H. Kavanah, The Responsible Society, Milton Keynes.
13. *Birth Control: Its Social, Political, Economic, Moral and Religious Aspects*, Abul 'Ala Mawdudi, Islamic Publications, Lahore, 1974.
14. *Fiqhus Sunnah* (Arabic, vols. I & II), As-Sayyid Sabiq, Darul Kitab Al-Arabi, Beirut, 1971.
15. *Nailul Awtar* (Arabic, vols. I & VI), Muhammad bin Ali Ibn Muhammad Ash-Shawkani, Dar Al-Jil, Beirut, 1973.
16. *Zadul Ma'ad* (Arabic, vol. IV), Ibn Qayyim, Muassasat Ar-Risalah, Beirut, 1979.
17. *Tarbiyatul 'Awlad Fil Islam* (Arabic, vol. I), Abdullah Nasihulwan, Darussalam, Beirut, 1981.